FILMING

Bewitched

"LOVE IS BLIND"

Filming Bewitched: Love is Blind by Chris Noel and Kirk Kimball
ISBN-13: 978-1500483326 - ISBN-10: 150048332X

Also by Chris Noel: "Matter of Survival: The War Jane Never Saw," "Vietnam and Me."
Also by Chris Noel and Kirk Kimball:
"Confessions of a Pin-Up Girl," "Filming Soldier in the Rain: Behind the Scenes with Steve McQueen
and Jackie Gleason," "Filming Girl Happy: Behind the Scenes with Elvis," "Filming The Glory Stompers:
Behind the Scenes with Dennis Hopper," "A Blonde Bomb Goes To Vietnam," and "Mary and Jesus."

CHRIS NOEL

EDITED AND DESIGNED BY KIRK KIMBALL

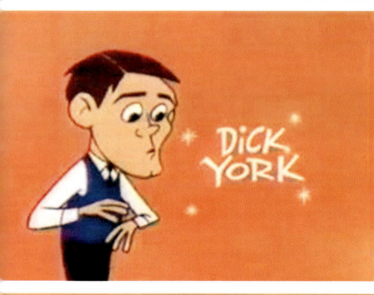
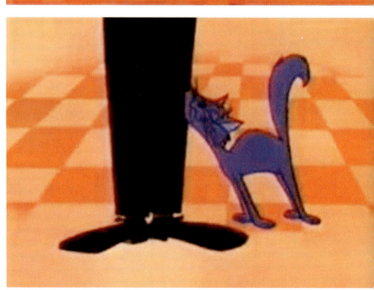

CONTENTS

On the left is William Asher, Liz Montgomery's husband. On the right is Dick York (Darrin) and Elizabeth Montgomery (Samantha).

Elizabeth Montgomery checks out the first issue of Dell's *Bewitched* comic book.

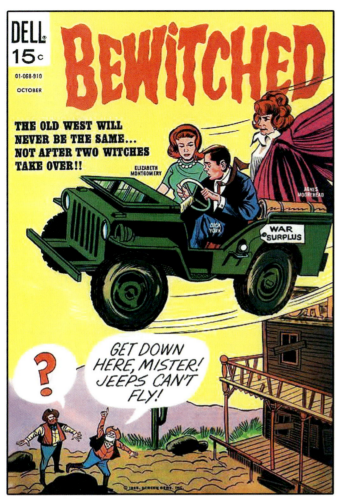

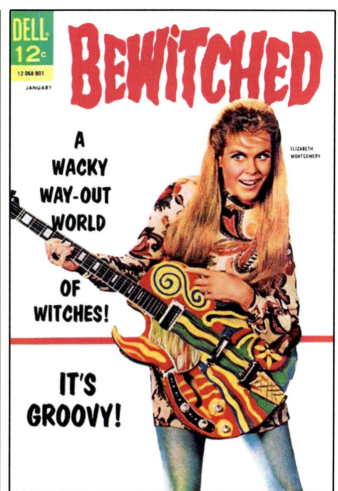

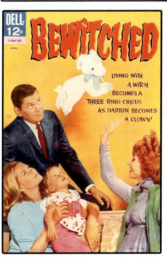

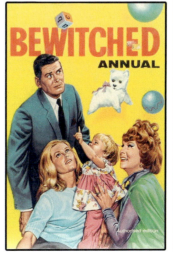

CASTING CALL

Liz Montgomery shrinks from a too-close clap board that lists her husband, William Asher as the episode's director.

ELIZABETH MONTGOMERY

LIKE everyone who watched TV in the Sixties, I loved the darling Elizabeth Montgomery. She started her career in the 1950s on her father's television series *Robert Montgomery Presents,* and landed the role of Samantha Stephens on ABC's *Bewitched* in 1964.

When I filmed my episode of the series, titled "Love is Blind," it was the 13th show of the series' very first season, but even then *Bewitched* was already a gigantic success. At the time, it was actually the biggest hit ABC ever had!

Liz seemed to have found the secret to success in Hollywood — marry your director. In 1963, Liz married William Asher, who directed the vast majority of *Bewitched* episodes for all eight seasons. They were married for the next ten years, and Liz had three children with Bill.

Another thing we have in common — Elvis! I went on to appear in several "beach party" movies, including *Girl Happy, Beach Ball,* and *Wild, Wild Winter.* So did Liz! She made a cameo appearance, spoofing her Samantha Stephens character, in the 1965 feature film comedy *How to Stuff a Wild Bikini,* which was (coincidence!) directed by her hubby, William Asher. And believe it or not, Liz also had an Elvis connection.

When her second husband, Gig Young, appeared in the Elvis movie *Kid Galahad* (1962), Liz visited the set constantly. When she began flirting with Elvis, Gig didn't like it one bit, and he screamed at her constantly. Elvis vowed never to work with him again. It was right after Liz divorced Gig that she married Bill Asher.

Elizabeth Montgomery passed away at age 62 in May 1995, due to complications cause by colorectal cancer. Following her passing, her 800-acre estate in Patterson, New York was sold to the state, and it has since been reopened as Wonder Lake State Park.

DICK YORK

D ICK York began his career at the age of 15 as the star of the CBS radio program *That Brewster Boy*. Following that, Dick appeared on hundreds of other radio shows. A turning point in his life came in 1959, while filming the western *They Came to Cordura*, Dick seriously injured his back while performing a stunt with co-star Gary Cooper. This started him down an endless road of painkillers and operations, and eventually ruined his career.

His chronic back pain got so bad the producers had to write Dick's injury into several of the *Bewitched* scripts, and in some of his final shows, Darrin is in bed or on a couch the entire episode. During season five, Dick passed out while filming one episode, and he finally decided to throw in the towel and quit the show.

He was replaced by Dick Sargent, the "other Darrin," without explanation, leading to decades of in-jokes about sitcom actors being interchangable. But actually, Dick Sargent had been offered the role of Darrin *before* Dick York. He'd turned it down, choosing to do an ABC sitcom called *Broadside*. That show only lasted one season, so when the time came, Sargent was free to take over as Darrin on *Bewitched* for the show's final seasons.

I remember Dick York as a wonderfully sweet man. If he was in pain during the filming of our episode, it was news to me. He always seemed so comfortable on the set, and he went out of his way to make *me* feel comfortable! That was very important to me, because I was just starting out in the business, and when you appear on a show as a guest star, you never really know how the cast is going to treat you until you actually do the show.

So the fact that an established star such as Dick York took the time to speak with me, and make me feel welcome on the *Bewitched* set, meant a great deal to me. And that's how I'll always remember Dick — as a wonderful, kind person, a hysterically funny comedian who was also a brilliant actor.

OPPOSITE PAGE:
Long-suffering Darrin gets an earful from Endora in "My What Big Ears You Have," Season 4, Episode 14, originally aired Dec. 7, 1967.

ADAM WEST

TODAY, everyone knows Adam West from his role as the title character in the 1966 *Batman* television series, but we filmed our episode of *Bewitched* in 1964, two years before *Batman*. At that time, Adam was only known as a hot, up-and-coming actor.

But it's a small world in Hollywood, and as it turns out, I had worked with Adam before we did *Bewitched*. We both appeared in *Soldier in the Rain*, a 1963 feature film starring Steve McQueen and Jackie Gleason. *Soldier* was my very first movie! Adam and I didn't have any scenes together in that film, but I spoke with him a few times on the set.

One time, Adam asked me about Gene Roddenberry. I knew Gene because I had done several episodes of his first TV show, before *Star Trek*. Called *The Lieutenant*, it was set on a Marine base in California. Adam asked about Gene because he wanted the role of Capt. Kirk, which Gene eventually gave another up-and-comer, Canadian William Shatner.

Adam and I had one more thing in common. As a member of the US Army, he been an announcer on American Forces Network Television. During the Vietnam War, I was a disk jockey for the Pentagon with my own hour-long daily radio program broadcast to the troops in Vietnam and around the world. As part of my job, I toured Vietnam several times during the war, and appeared on American Forces Network television many times, to entertain the troops.

So I was happy when I learned that Adam West would be appearing in my *Bewitched* episode, and although we had never had any romantic encounters, I was looking forward to playing one of his former girlfriends!

Today, at age 85, Adam is still very active in show business. In addition to appearing in feature films, he also does tons of voice-over work for animated series such as *The Fairly OddParents* and *Family Guy*, where he does the voices for a crazy, deranged fictional versions of himself.

And, believe it or not, Adam West still does Batman! He's done voice-over work for several animated Batman-related televisions series, such as *The New Adventures of Batman, Batman The Animated Series,* and *Batman: The Brave and The Bold.*

RIGHT: Adam West as Batman by Mike Allred.

CHRIS NOEL

I STARTED as a model in West Palm Beach, Florida, and broke into show business with the help of actor Hugh O'Brian. Then I landed a role in the Steve McQueen film *Soldier in the Rain*, which also featured Adam West in a small role. After that, I had the pleasure of appearing in *Girl Happy* with the King of Rock 'n' Roll, Elvis Presley.

In 1965, I joined the Governor of California, baseball legend Sandy Koufax and others in touring Letterman Hospital in California. I put on a happy face while visiting the gangrene ward, but the condition of the Vietnam vets there shocked me deeply. It was a life-changing experience.

I vowed to do something to help our servicemen, and fulfilled my vow when the Pentagon hired me to do a daily, hour-long radio show broadcast to our troops in Vietnam and around the world. My AFRTS radio program was called *A Date With Chris*, and I opened each program by saying, "Hi love!"

In 1967, I told the *National Enquirer*, "I'm just a girl who's trying to make the men she loves happy. You see, I'm in love with half-a-million guys — all the American troops in Vietnam."

I visited Vietnam many times during Christmas, so they called me "Miss Christmas," but when I shot my episode of *Bewitched, "Love is Blind,"* on Thursday, October 29, 1964, I was just thrilled to be on a hit show, and had no idea what lay ahead for me.

LEFT: Chris Noel from Marvel Comics' *The Nam* **#23 (Oct. 1988)**
BELOW: *The Hollywood Reporter* **news item, October 28, 1964.**

THE HOLLYWOOD REPORTER

Chris Noel Guest Stars In 'Love is Blind' Segment

Chris Noel has been signed to guest-star in "Love Is Blind," telefilm in Screen Gems' "Bewitched" series. Miss Noel checks in tomorrow to director William Asher. Danny Arnold produces with Elizabeth Montgomery, Dick York and Agnes Moorehead co-starring.

KIT SMYTHE

LEGENDARY Hollywood producer Sherwood Schwartz, creator of *The Brady Bunch*, *My Favorite Martian*, and many other memorable shows, gave Kit Smythe her first television acting job when he cast her as "Ginger Grant" in the pilot episode of *Gilligan's Island*.

Originally, the Ginger character was supposed to be a secretary. But when the pilot became a TV series, Ginger's backstory was changed to make her an actress, and Kit was replaced by Tina Louise.

Kit's mother and grandmother were both actresses, and she appeared in her first Broadway show at age 21. Following the *Gilligan's Island* pilot, Kit also did several other sitcoms, including *The Farmer's Daughter* and *The Bob Newhart Show*, and she also played dramatic roles on *Gunsmoke*, *Police Woman*, and *Burke's Law*. Coincidentally, I myself appeared on two different episodes of *Burke's Law*, playing two different characters.

In our episode of *Bewitched*, "Love is Blind," Kit plays Gertrude, Samantha's unmarried girlfriend. Sam convinces Darrin to set Gertrude up with one of his co-workers at the McMann and Tate Ad Agency — a handsome Bachelor named Kermit, played by Adam West. The typically whacky sitcom hijinks begin when Darrin starts to believe that Kit is secretly a witch, like Samantha, and, to Samantha's distress, he gets me (Chris Noel) to help break up the couple.

LEFT: Adam West and Kit Smythe in Bewitched, "Love is Blind."

BEWITCHED

THE PARTRIDGE FAMILY

I DREAM OF JEANIE

LETHAL WEAPON

BRIAN'S SONG

NL'S CHRISTMAS VACATION

PEE WEE'S BIG ADVENTURE

HOME IMPROVEMENT

The *Bewitched* house as it appeared in *Our Man Higgins.*

THE *Bewitched* HOUSE

THE Bewitched house (pictured above), said to be located on 1164 Morning Glory Circle, was the home of Samantha and Darrin Stephens from 1964-1972. It's part of an area known as the Warner Bros. Ranch, and it's called "Blondie Street" because several of the homes there were originally constructed for the *Blondie* movie series, based on the *Blondie* comc strip by Chic Young.

The Bewitched house was originally constructed in July 1962 for the short-lived sitcom *Our Man Higgins*, which starred Stanley Holloway as a butler. In addition to *Bewitched*, the home has also appeared in many other television shows and feature films, as pictured on the opposite page.

Like all the houses on this block, the Stephens house is actually just an empty fascade. Several

The Bewitched House is actually a realistic facade that's small and empty inside. The photo above shows the inside of the house looking out to the street.

Bewitched

Bewitched

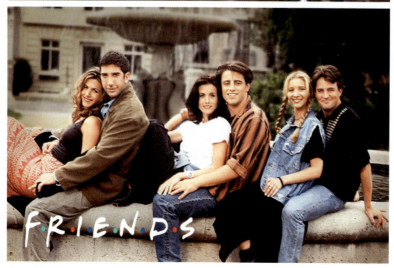

FRIENDS

Bewitched scenes were shot in the set's park area, near the same fountain where the *Friends* frolic during that show's opening title sequence (as pictured on the left).

Pictured on the upper right of the photo on the opposite page is a small church, which appeared in my episode of *Bewitched* as the place Gertrude and Kermit (Adam West) get married.

At the time we shot *Love is Blind*, this church was right across the street from the Stephen's house. It's still on the street, but not in the same place. Since it's just a fasade, it was easy to pick it up and move it back a bit. You can see it in the upper right corner of the photo on the opposite page.

The homes on Blondie Street have been destroyed several times by various fires, but they have always been rebuilt. The *Bewitched* home was destroyed by a fire in 1970, but it was reconstructed and still stands today, remaining a popular part of the Warner Bros. Ranch tour.

1 NATIONAL LAMPOON's CHRISTMAS VACATION

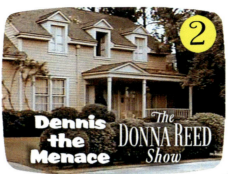

2 Dennis the Menace · The DONNA REED Show

3 Bewitched

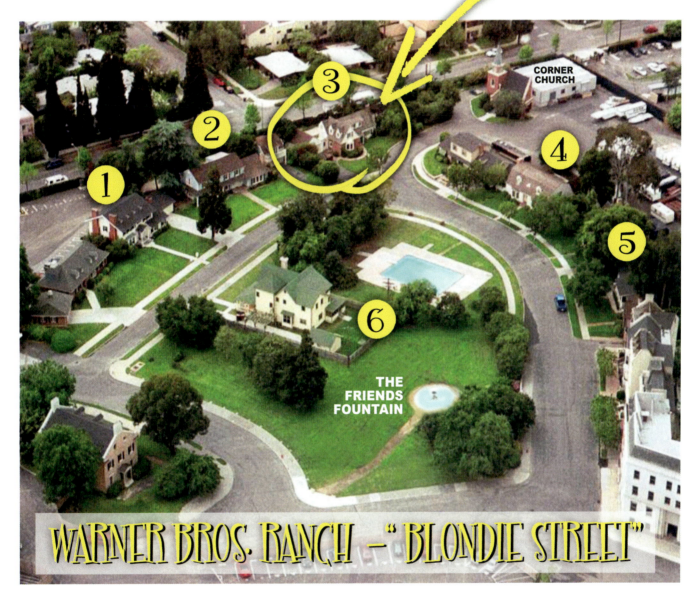

CORNER CHURCH

THE FRIENDS FOUNTAIN

WARNER BROS. RANCH — "BLONDIE STREET"

4 the partridge family

5 I DREAM of JEANNIE

6 PROJECT X

M^CMANN & TATE ADVERTISING

IN my episode of *Bewitched*, I was playing a model. Rather than go out and have some "model type" photographs taken of me, the producers asked If I had any they could use. As a former model, I had tons! I showed them several, and they picked the ones seen above, and on the opposite page.

In the scenes pictured below, which take place at McMann & Tate Advertising (where Darrin works), Kermit (Adam West), supposedly a former boyfriend of mine, is touching-up pictures of me for a magazine advertisement when Darrin (Dick York) asks him to double-date with himself, Samantha, and Susan (me, Chris Noel). Kermit doesn't really want to go, but Darrin talks him into it.

Bewitched

D ARRIN calls and invites me to dinner with himself, Samantha, and Kermit (Adam). Yes, I know it's a stupid name, especially for someone who would go on to play Batman! I mean, Bruce Wayne, OK, but *Kermit?* Was he named after Kermit the frog or something? Whatever.

Anyway, when I get Darrin's call, the scene looks as if my bedroom is set up for a Playboy photo shoot. I'm wearing nothing but a pink silk outfit, cinched at the waist with a pom-pom string. I'm talking on a gold-encrusted telephone — a dial up! Remember those? And the bed is covered with blue silk sheets. It looks like I'm posing for a magazine layout.

Back to the call. I say, "I remember you Darrin, you work with that treacherous Kermit, who hasn't called me in more than a month! A spell? Well, if he's been sick, I'm sure I can make him feel better. All right... The Interlude at 10:00. I'll be there."

T HE reason Darrin is going to all this trouble is because he thinks Kit is secretly a witch, and that she's being dishonest with Kermit by not telling him. Darrin knew I had a previous relationship with Kermit from their work at the ad agency, so I was a convenient way to distract Kermit. He was planning on using me frustrate Samantha's matchmaking!

The producers explained to me that this was a main theme of the show was the problem many men have dealing with powerful women. Darrin represents the everyman dealing with a plethora of powerful women, including his magical wife as well as her mother, Endora (played brilliantly by Agnes Moorehead, who unfortunately wasn't in my episode), and an endless array of kooky relatives.

Bewitched is based on the 1942 movie *I Married a Witch*, starring Veronica Lake, and the 1958 film *Bell, Book, and Candle* with James Stewart and Kim Novak.

Liz Montgomery, Adam West, Chris Noel and Dick York in the "Love is Blind" dinner scene.

A Bewitching DINNER DATE

SO, we all get together at "The Interlude" for a dinner date. My hair was all done up with wires (for a certain special effect). I wore my own gorgeous mink stole (a present from a former boyfriend), and they gave me a red velvet dress with two thin straps — also wired for another "magical" effect.

I walk into the restaurant, and right away Samantha is not happy to see me. She knows Darrin is up to something!

At first, everything goes really well. Kermit and I have a few laughs remembering old times. But when Samantha sees us connecting, she uses her famous "nose-twitch" magic to make me suddenly get furiously angry with poor, unsuspecting Kermit! It was a dream

scene for an actress, because in the space of a few minutes I go from a giggly, almost drunken happiness, to a sudden, inexplicable fury. Then I storm out of the restaurant!

After I leave, Sam's spell wears off and I decide to return to the table, but she sees me approaching.

With another few twitches (actually Liz was just moving her mouth, and her nose followed along), she first causes the straps on my gown to burst, then sends my hairdo flying apart. Crew members pulled on invisible wires to make the magic spell work.

And it did work! In the end, Kermit marries Gertude (Kit Smythe) — just as Sam planned all along. Here are some still frames...

Kermit (Adam) and I are enjoying our double date with the Stephens...

until Samantha uses her magic "twitch" to make me furious with Kermit.

Then, as I storm out, Samantha suddenly sends my hairdo flying apart!

Bewitched

The episode ends with Darrin and Samantha watching as Kermit and Gertrude get married.

The exterior seen above is a church fascade on Blondie Street, the place that really has everything.

ABOVE:
Back home, Darrin and Samantha kiss and make-up.

LEFT:
Credit from the episode. Chris Noel got third billing, right under the show's two lead stars.

Bewitched

Bewitched

Bewitched

Bewitched

Bewitched

Bewitched

Bewitched FIFTY YEARS LATER

BEWITCHED is just one of those shows! It was a product of its era — but somehow, even fifty years later, it still feels absolutely contemporary.

And the show hasn't faded away into television oblivion. It's still a perennial best-seller on DVD, and it airs almost every night on several different cable TV stations across America, and the world.

That's because, for all its magical hijinks, the show is really about the relationship between men and women. And to this day, it's one of the very few shows to ever portray a relationship where the female is so clearly dominant that the male is constantly threatened by her.

A scary prospect for many men, perhaps, but for girls and women who grew up watching *Bewitched*, it was a great relief to know that Batman, Superman, and every other MAN weren't the only ones who could have special abilities... so could WOMEN!

And, in the case of *Bewitched*, the results were never so hilarious, and at the same time so heartwarming.

PICTURED above are some of the greatest *Bewitched* fans in the entire world, posing in front of 1164 Morning Glory Circle, the former residence of the Stephens family, in July 2014.

Samantha, Darrin, Tabitha and Adam moved out years ago, but don't worry. They left a forwarding address. You can see them in their new permanent residence: TV Land.

Chris Noel materializes in front of the BEWITCHED House for Bewitched Fanfare July 2014.

BEWITCHED FANFARE 2014

OPPOSITE PAGE:
Erin Murphy (Tabitha) and Bernard Fox (Dr. Bombay).

ABOVE/LEFT:
Kit Smythe and Chris Noel take questions from the audience.

Printed in Great Britain
by Amazon